Briefly About Disagreements in the Party
Joseph Stalin

Prism Key Press, 2013.
New York, NY.

ISBN-10:1489558780
ISBN-13:978-1489558787

Briefly About Disagreements in the Party

Joseph Stalin

"We think that a powerful and vigorous movement is impossible without differences — 'true conformity' is possible only in the cemetery. " - J.V. Stalin (*Pravda*, 1912).

Briefly About Disagreements in the Party

"Social-Democracy is a combination of the working-class movement with socialism." — Karl Kautsky

Our "Mensheviks" are really too tiresome! I am referring to the Tiflis "Mensheviks." They heard that there are disagreements in the Party and so they began harping: whether you like it or not we shall talk about disagreements, always and everywhere; whether you like it or not we shall abuse the "Bolsheviks" right and left! And so they are hurling abuse for all they are worth, as if they are possessed. At all the crossroads, among themselves and among strangers, in short, wherever they happen to be, they howl one thing: beware of the "majority," they are strangers, infidels! Not content with the "habitual" field, they have carried the "case" into the legally published literature, thereby proving to the world once again . . . how tiresome they are.

What has the "majority" done? Why is our "minority" so "wrathful"?

Let us turn to history.

* * *

The "majority" and "minority" first came into being at the Second Party Congress (1903). That was the congress at which our scattered forces were to have united in one powerful

7

party. We Party workers placed great hopes in that congress. At last!—we exclaimed joyfully—we, too, shall be united in one party, we, too, shall be able to work according to a single plan! . . . It goes without saying that we had been active before that, but our activities were scattered and unorganised. It goes without saying that we had made attempts to unite before that; it was for this purpose that we convened the First Party Congress (1898), and it even looked as if we had "united," but this unity existed in name only: the Party still remained split up into separate groups; our forces still remained scattered and had yet to be united. And so the Second Party Congress was to have mustered our scattered forces and united them in one whole. We were to have formed a united party.

Actually it turned out, however, that our hopes had been to some degree premature. The congress failed to give us a single and indivisible party; it merely laid the foundation for such a party. The congress did, however, clearly reveal to us that there are two trends within the Party: the *Iskra* trend (I mean the old *Iskra*), and the trend of its opponents. Accordingly, the congress split up into two sections: into a "majority" and a "minority." The former joined the *Iskra* trend and rallied around that paper; the latter, being opponents of *Iskra*, took the opposite stand.

Thus, *Iskra* became the banner of the Party "majority," and *Iskra*'s stand became the stand of the "majority."

What path did *Iskra* take? What did it advocate?

To understand this one must know the conditions under which it entered the historical field.

Iskra started publication in December 1900. That was the time when a crisis began in Russian industry. The industrial boom, which was accompanied by a number of economic strikes (1896-98), gradually gave way to a crisis. The crisis grew more acute day by day and became an obstacle to economic strikes. In spite of that, the working-class movement hewed a path for itself and made progress; the individual streams merged in a single flood; the movement acquired a class aspect and gradually took the path of the political struggle. The working-class movement grew with astonishing rapidity. . . . But there was no sign of an advanced detachment, no Social-Democracy which would have introduced socialist consciousness into the movement, would have combined it with socialism, and, thereby, would have lent the proletarian struggle a Social-Democratic character.

What did the "Social-Democrats" of that time (they were called "Economists") do? They burned incense to the spontaneous movement and light-heartedly reiterated: socialist consciousness is not so very necessary for the working-class movement, which can very well reach its goal without it; the main thing is the movement. The movement is everything— consciousness is a mere trifle. *A movement without socialism —* that was what they were striving for.

In that case, what is the mission of Russian Social-Democracy? Its mission is to be an obedient tool of the spontaneous movement, they asserted. It is not our business to introduce socialist consciousness into the working-class movement, it is not our business to lead this movement—that would be fruitless coercion; our duty is merely to watch the movement and take careful note of what goes on in social life— we must drag at the tail of the spontaneous movement. In short, *Social-Democracy* was depicted as *an unnecessary burden* on the movement.

Whoever refuses to recognise Social-Democracy must also refuse to recognise the Social-Democratic Party.

That is precisely why the "Economists" so persistently reiterated that a proletarian political party could not exist in Russia. Let the liberals engage in the political struggle, it is more fitting for them to do so, said the "Economists." But what must we Social-Democrats do? We must continue to exist as separate circles, each operating isolatedly in its own corner.

9

Not a Party, but a circle! *they said.*

Thus, on the one hand, the working-class movement grew and stood in need of a guiding advanced detachment; on the other hand, "Social-Democracy," represented by the "Economists," instead of taking the lead of the movement, abnegated itself and dragged at the tail of the movement.

It was necessary to proclaim for all to hear the idea that a spontaneous working-class movement without socialism means groping in the dark, and, even if it ever does lead to the goal, who knows how long it will take, and at what cost in suffering; that, consequently, socialist consciousness is of enormous importance for the working-class movement.

It was also necessary to proclaim that it is the duty of the vehicle of this consciousness, Social-Democracy, to imbue the working-class movement with socialist consciousness; to be always at the head of the movement and not to be a mere observer of the spontaneous working-class movement, not to drag at its tail.

It was also necessary to express the idea that it is the direct duty of Russian Social-Democracy to muster the separate advanced detachments of the proletariat, to unite them in one party, and thereby to put an end to disunity in the Party once and for all.

It was precisely these tasks that *Iskra* proceeded to formulate.

This is what it said in its programmatic article (see *Iskra*, No. 1): "Social-Democracy is a combination of the working-class movement with socialism," i.e., the movement without socialism, or socialism standing aloof from the movement, is an undesirable state of affairs which

Social-Democracy must combat. But as the "Economists-*Rabocheye Delo*-ists" worshipped the spontaneous movement, and as they belittled the importance of socialism, *Iskra* stated: "Isolated from Social-Democracy, the working-class movement becomes petty and inevitably becomes bourgeois." Consequently, it is the duty of Social-Democracy "to point out to this movement its ultimate aim and its political tasks, and to guard its political and ideological independence."

What are the duties of Russian Social-Democracy? "From this," continues *Iskra*, "automatically emerges the task which it is the mission of Russian Social-Democracy to fulfil: to imbue the masses of the proletariat with the ideas of socialism and with political consciousness and to organise a revolutionary party that will be inseverably connected with the spontaneous working-class movement," — i.e., it must always be at the head of the movement, and its paramount duty is to unite the Social-Democratic forces of the working-class movement in one party.

That is how the editorial board of *Iskra* formulated its programme.

Did *Iskra* carry out this splendid programme?

Everybody knows how devotedly it put these extremely important ideas into practice. That was clearly demonstrated to us by the Second Party Congress, at which the majority, numbering 35 votes, recognised *Iskra* as the central organ of the Party.

Is it not ridiculous, after that, to hear certain pseudo-Marxists "berate" the old *Iskra*?

This is what the Menshevik Social-Democrat writes about *Iskra*:

"It (*Iskra*) should have analysed the ideas of 'Economism,' rejected its fallacious views and accepted its correct ones, and directed it into a new channel. . . . *But that did not happen.* The fight against 'Economism' gave rise to another extreme: the economic struggle was belittled and treated with disdain; supreme importance was attached to the political struggle. *Politics without economy* (it ought to be: "without economics")— such is the new trend" (see Social-Democrat, No . 1, "Majority or Minority?").

11

But when, where, in what country did all this happen, highly esteemed "critic"? What did Plekhanov, Axelrod, Zasulich, Martov and Starover do? Why did they not turn *Iskra* to the "true" path? Did they not constitute the majority on the editorial board? And where have you yourself been up to now, my dear sir? Why did you not warn the Second Party Congress? It would not then have recognised *Iskra* as the central organ.

But let us leave the "critic."

The point is that *Iskra* correctly emphasised the "urgent questions of the day"; it took the path I spoke about above and devotedly carried out its programme.

Iskra's stand was still more distinctly and convincingly formulated by Lenin, in his splendid book *What Is To Be Done?*

Let us deal with this book.

The "Economists" worshipped the spontaneous working-class movement; but who does not know that the spontaneous movement is a movement without socialism, that it "is trade unionism" which refuses to see anything beyond the limits of capitalism. Who does not know that the working-class movement without socialism means marking time within the limits of capitalism, wandering around private property, and, even if this ever does lead to the social revolution, who knows how long it will take, and at what cost in suffering? Does it make no difference to the workers whether they enter the "promised land" in the near future or after a long period of time; by an easy or by a difficult road? Clearly, whoever extols the *spontaneous* movement and worships it, whether he wishes to or not, digs a chasm between socialism and the working-class movement, belittles the importance of socialist ideology and expels it from life, and, whether he wishes to or not, subordinates the workers to bourgeois ideology; for he fails to understand that "Social-Democracy is a combination of the working-class movement with socialism," that *"all* worship of the spontaneity of the working-class movement, *all* belittling of

12

the role of 'the conscious element,' of the role of Social-Democracy, *means, quite irrespective of whether the belittler wants to or not, strengthening the influence of bourgeois ideology over the workers."*

To explain this in greater detail: In our times only two ideologies can exist: bourgeois and socialist. The difference between them is, among other things, that the former, i.e., bourgeois ideology, is much older, more widespread and more deep-rooted in life than the latter; that one encounters bourgeois views everywhere, in one's own and in other circles, whereas socialist ideology is only taking its first steps, is only just hewing a road for itself. Needless to say, as regards the spread of ideas, bourgeois ideology, i.e., trade-unionist consciousness, spreads far more easily and embraces the *spontaneous* working-class movement far more widely than socialist ideology, which is only taking its first steps. That is all the more true for the reason that, even as it is, the *spontaneous* movement—the movement without socialism —"leads to its becoming subordinated to bourgeois ideology." And subordination to bourgeois ideology means ousting socialist ideology, because one is the negation of the other.

We shall be asked: But surely the working class gravitates towards socialism? Yes, it gravitates towards socialism. *If it did not, the activities of Social-Democracy would be fruitless.* But it is also true that this gravitation is counteracted and hindered by another—gravitation towards bourgeois ideology.

I have just said that our social life is impregnated with bourgeois ideas and, consequently; it is much easier to spread bourgeois ideology than socialist ideology. It must not be forgotten that meanwhile the bourgeois ideologists are not asleep; they, in their own way, disguise themselves as Socialists and are tireless in their efforts to subordinate the working class to bourgeois ideology. If, under these circumstances, the Social-Democrats, too, like the "Economists," go woolgatheringand drag at the tail of the spontaneous movement (and the working-class movement is spontaneous when Social-Democracy behaves that way), then it is self-evident that the spontaneous working-class movement will proceed along that beaten path and submit to bourgeois ideology until, of course, long wanderings and sufferings compel it to break with bourgeois ideology and strive for the social revolution.

It is this that is called gravitating towards bourgeois ideology .

Here is what Lenin says:

"The working class spontaneously gravitates towards socialism, but the more widespread (and continuously revived in the most diverse forms) bourgeois ideology nevertheless spontaneously imposes itself upon the working class still more." This is precisely why the *spontaneous* working-class movement, while it is *spontaneous,* while it is not yet combined with socialist consciousness—becomes subordinated to bourgeois ideology and gravitates towards such subordination. *If that were not the case, Social-Democratic criticism, Social-Democratic propaganda, would be superfluous, and it would be unnecessary to "combine the working-class movement with socialism."*

It is the duty of Social-Democracy to *combat* this gravitation towards bourgeois ideology and to stimulate the other gravitation—gravitation towards socialism. Some day, of course, after long wanderings and sufferings, the spontaneous movement would come into its own,would arrive at the gates of the social revolution, without the aid of Social-Democracy, because "the working class spontaneously gravitates towards socialism." But what is to happen in the meantime, what shall we do in the meantime? Fold our arms across our chests as the "Economists" do and leave the field to the Struves and Zubatovs? Renounce Social-Democracy and thereby help bourgeois, trade-unionist ideology to predominate? Forget Marxism and not "combine socialism with the working-class

14

movement"?

No! Social-Democracy is the advanced detachment of the proletariat, and its duty is always to be at the head of the proletariat; its duty is "to divert the working-class movement from this spontaneous, trade-unionist tendency to come under the wing of the bourgeoisie, and to bring it under the wing of revolutionary Social-Democracy." The duty of Social-Democracy is to imbue the spontaneous working-class movement with socialist consciousness, to combine the working-class movement with socialism and thereby lend the proletarian struggle a Social-Democratic character.

It is said that in some countries the working *class* itself worked out the socialist ideology (scientific socialism) and will itself work it out in other countries too, and that, therefore, it is unnecessary to introduce socialist consciousness into the working-class movement from without. But this is a profound mistake. To be able to work out the theory of scientific socialism onemust stand at the head of science, one must be armed with scientific knowledge and be able deeply to investigate the laws of historical development. But the working *class,* while it remains a working class, is unable to stand in the van of science, to advance it and investigate scientifically the laws of history; it lacks both the time and the means for that. Scientific socialism "can arise only on the basis of profound scientific knowledge. . ." — says K. Kautsky. ". . . The vehicle of science is not the proletariat, but the *bourgeois intelligentsia (K. Kautsky's italics)*. It was in the minds of individual members of that stratum that modern socialism originated, and it was they who communicated it to the more intellectually developed proletarians. . . ."

Accordingly, Lenin says: All those who worship the spontaneous working-class movement and look on with folded arms, those who continuously belittle the importance of Social-Democracy and leave the field to the Struves and Zubatovs — all imagine that this movement itself works out scientific

15

socialism. "But that is a profound mistake." Some people believe that the St. Petersburg workers who went on strike in the nineties possessed Social-Democratic consciousness, but that, too, is a mistake. There was no such consciousness among them and "there could not be. It (Social-Democratic consciousness) could be brought to them only from without. The history of all countries shows that the workingclass, exclusively by its own efforts, is able to develop only trade-unionist consciousness, i.e., the conviction that it is necessary to combine in unions, fight the employers and strive to compel the government to pass necessary labour legislation, etc. The theory of socialism, however, grew out of the philosophic, historical and economic theories that were elaborated by the educated representatives of the propertied classes, the intellectuals. According to their social status, the founders of modern scientific socialism, Marx and Engels, themselves belonged to the bourgeois intelligentsia." That does not mean, of course, continues Lenin, "that the workers have no part in creating such an ideology. But they take part not as workers, but as socialist theoreticians, as Proudhons and Weitlings (both were working men); in other words, they take part only when, and to the extent that they are able, more or less, to acquire the knowledge of their age and advance that knowledge."

We can picture all this to ourselves approximately as follows. There is a capitalist system. There are workers and masters. Between them a struggle is raging. So far there are no signs whatever of scientific socialism. Scientific socialism was not even thought of anywhere when the workers were already waging their struggle. . . . Yes, the workers are fighting. But they are fighting separately against their masters; they come into collision with their local authorities; here they go out on strike, there they hold meetings and demonstrations; here they demand rights from the government, there they proclaim a boycott; some talk about the political struggle, others about the economic struggle, and so forth. But that does not mean that the workers possess Social-Democratic consciousness; it does not

16

mean that the aim of their movement is to overthrow the capitalist system, that they are as sure of the overthrow of capitalism and of the establishment of the socialist system as they are of the inevitable rising of the sun, that they regard their conquest of political power (the dictatorship of the proletariat) as an essential means for achieving the victory of socialism, etc.

Meanwhile science develops. The working-class movement gradually attracts its attention. Most scientists arrive at the opinion that the working-class movement is a revolt of troublemakers whom it would be a good thing to bring to their senses with the aid of the whip. Others believe that it is the duty of the rich to throw some crumbs to the poor, i.e., that the working-class movement is a movement of paupers whose object is to obtain alms. And out of a thousand scientists perhaps only one may prove to be a man who approaches the working-class movement scientifically, scientifically investigates the whole of social life, watches the conflict of classes, listens closely to the murmuring of the working class and, finally, proves scientifically that the capitalist system is by no means eternal, that it is just as transient as feudalism was, and that it must inevitably be superseded by its negation, the socialist system, which can be established only by the proletariat by means of a social revolution. In short, scientific socialism is elaborated.

It goes without saying that if there were no capitalism and the class struggle there would he no scientific socialism. But it is also true that these few, for example Marx and Engels, would not have worked out scientific socialism had they not possessed scientific knowledge.

What is scientific socialism *without the working-class movement?* — A compass which, if left unused, will only grow rusty and then will have to be thrown overboard.

What is the working-class movement *without socialism*? —A ship without a compass which will reach the other shore in any case, but would reach it much sooner and with less danger

17

if it had a compass.

Combine the two and you will get a splendid vessel, which will speed straight towards the other shore and reach its haven unharmed.

Combine the working-class movement with socialism and you will get a Social-Democratic movement which will speed straight towards the "promised land."

And so, it is the duty of Social-Democracy (and not only of Social-Democratic intellectuals) to combine socialism with the working-class movement, to imbue the movement with socialist consciousness and thereby lend the spontaneous working-class movement a Social-Democratic character.

That is what Lenin says.

Some people assert that in the opinion of Lenin and the "majority," the working-class movement will perish, will fail to achieve the social revolution if it is not combined with socialist ideology. That is an invention, the invention of idle minds, which could have entered the heads only of pseudo-Marxists like An (see "What Is a Party?", *Mogzauri* No. 6).

Lenin says definitely that "The working class spontaneously gravitates towards socialism," and if he does not dwell on this at great length, it is only because he thinks it unnecessary to prove what has already been proved. Moreover, Lenin did not set out to investigate the *spontaneous* movement; he merely wanted to show those engaged in practical Party work what they ought to do *consciously*.

Here is what Lenin says in another passage in his controversy with Martov:

"'Our Party is the conscious exponent of an unconscious process.' Exactly. And for this very reason it is wrong to want 'every striker' to have the right to call himself a Party member, for if 'every strike' were not only a spontaneous expression of a powerful *class instinct and of the class struggle, which is*

18

inevitably leading to the social revolution, but a conscious expression of that process . . . then our Party . . . would at once put an end to the entire bourgeois society."

As you see, in Lenin's opinion, even the class struggle and the class conflicts which cannot be called Social-Democratic, nevertheless inevitably lead the working class to the social revolution.

If you are interested to hear the opinion of other representatives of the "majority," here is what one of them, Comrade Gorin, said at the Second Party Congress:

"What would the situation be if the proletariat were left to itself? It would be similar to what it was on theeve of the bourgeois revolution. The bourgeois revolutionaries had no scientific ideology. The bourgeois system came into being nevertheless. Even without ideologists the proletariat would, of course, in the long run, work towards the social revolution, but it would do so instinctively. . . . Instinctively the proletariat would practise socialism, but it would lack socialist theory. Only, the process would be slow and more painful."

Further explanation is superfluous.

Thus, the spontaneous working-class movement, the working-class movement *without socialism,* inevitably becomes petty and assumes a trade-unionist character—it submits to bourgeois ideology. Can we draw the conclusion from this that socialism is everything and the working-class movement nothing? Of course not! Only idealists say that. Some day, in the far distant future, economic development will inevitably bring the working class to the social revolution, and, consequently, compel it to break off all connection with bourgeois ideology. The only point is that this path is a very long and painful one.

On the other hand, socialism *without the working-class movement,* no matter on what scientific basis it may have arisen, nevertheless remains an empty phrase and loses its significance. Can we draw the conclusion from this that the movement is

19

everything and socialism — nothing? Of course not! Only pseudo-Marxists, who attach no importance to consciousness because it is engendered by social life itself, argue that way. Socialism can becombined with the working-class movement and thereby be transformed from an empty phrase into a sharp weapon.

The conclusion?

The conclusion is that the working-class movement must be combined with socialism; practical activities and theoretical thought must merge into one and thereby lend the spontaneous working-class movement a Social-Democratic character, for "Social-Democracy is a combination of the working-class movement with socialism." Then, socialism, combined with the working-class movement, will, in the hands of the workers, be transformed from an empty phrase into a tremendous force. Then, the spontaneous movement, transformed into a Social-Democratic movement, will march rapidly along the true road to the socialist system.

What, then, is the mission of Russian Social-Democracy? What must we do?

Our duty, the duty of Social-Democracy, is to deflect the spontaneous working-class movement from the path of narrow trade unionism to the Social-Democratic path. Our duty is to introduce socialist consciousness into this movement and unite the advanced forces of the working class in one centralised party. Our task is always to be at the head of the movement and combat tirelessly all those—whether they be foes or "friends"—who hinder the accomplishment of this task.

Such, in general, is the position of the "majority."

Our "minority" dislikes the position taken by the "majority"; it is "un-Marxist," it says; it "fundamentally contradicts" Marxism! But is that so, most highly esteemed gentlemen? Where, when, on what planet? Read our articles, they say, and you will be convinced that we are right. Very well, let us read them.

We have before us an article entitled "What Is a Party?" (see *Mogzauri,* No. 6). Of what does the "critic" An accuse the Party "majority"? "It (the "majority") . . . proclaims itself the head of the Party . . . and demands submission from others . . . and to justify its conduct it often even invents new theories, such as, for example, that the working people cannot by their own efforts *assimilate (my italics)* 'lofty ideals,'etc."

The question now is: Does the "majority" advance, or has it ever advanced, such "theories"? Never! Nowhere! On the contrary, Comrade Lenin, the ideological representative of the "majority," very definitely says that the working class very easily *assimilates* "lofty ideals," that it very easily *assimilates* socialism. Listen:

"It is often said: the working class *spontaneously* gravitates towards socialism. This is perfectly true in the sense that socialist theory defines the causes of the misery of the working class more profoundly and more correctly than any other theory, and for that reason the *workers are able to assimilate it so easily.*"

As you see, in the opinion of the "majority," the workers easily assimilate the "lofty ideals" which are called socialism.

So what is An getting at? Where did he dig up his queer "find"? The point is, reader, that "critic" An had something entirely different in mind. He had in mind that passage in *What Is To Be Done?* where Lenin speaks of the *elaboration* of the theory of socialism, where he says that the working class *cannot elaborate* scientific socialism by its own efforts. But how is that?—you will ask. To *elaborate* the theory of socialism is one thing —to *assimilate* it is another. Why did An forget those words of Lenin's in which he so clearly speaks of the *assimilation* of "lofty ideals"? You are right, reader, but what can An do since he is so anxious to be a "critic"? Just think what a heroic deed he is performing: he invents a "theory" of his own, ascribes it to his opponent, and then bombards the fruit of his own imagination! That is criticism, if you like! At all events it is beyond doubt that An "could not by his own efforts assimilate" Lenin's book *What Is To Be Done?*

Let us now open the so-called *Social-Democrat.* What does the author of the article "Majority or Minority?" (see Social-Democrat, No. 1) say?

Plucking up courage, he vociferously attacks Lenin for expressin g the opinion that the "natural (it ought to be "spontaneous") development of the working-class movement leads not to socialism, but to bourgeois ideology." The author evidently fails to understand that the *spontaneous* working-class movement is a movement without socialism (let the author prove that this is not so), and that such a movement inevitably submits to bourgeois trade-unionist ideology, gravitates towards it; for in our times there can be only two ideologies, socialist and bourgeois, and where the former is absent the latter inevitably appears and occupies its place (prove the opposite!). Yes, this is exactly what Lenin says. But at the same time he does not forget about another gravitation that is characteristic of the working-class movement—gravitation towards socialism, which is only temporarily eclipsed by the gravitation towards bourgeois ideology. Lenin says definitely that "the working class spontaneously gravitates towards socialism," and he rightly observes that it is the duty of Social-Democracy to accelerate the victory of this gravitation by, among other things, combating the "Economists." Why, then, esteemed "critic," did you not quote these words of Lenin in your article? Were they not uttered by the very same Lenin? Because it was not to your advantage. Isn't that so?

"In Lenin's opinion . . . the worker, owing to his *position (my italics),* is a bourgeois rather than a Socialist . . . " — continues the author. Well! I didn't expect anything so stupid even from such an author! Does Lenin talk about the worker's *position*? Does he say that owing to his *position* the worker is a bourgeois? Who but an idiot can say that owing to his *position* the worker is a bourgeois — the worker who owns no means of production and lives by selling his labour power? No! Lenin says something entirely different. The point is that owing to my *position* I can be a proletarian and not a bourgeois, but at the same time I can be unconscious of my *position* and, as a consequence, submit to bourgeois ideology. This is exactly how the matter stands in this case with the working class. And it means something entirely different.

In general, the author is fond of hurling empty phrases about—he shoots them off without thinking! Thus, for example, the author obstinately reiterates that "Leninism fundamentally contradicts Marxism"; he reiterates this and fails to see where this "idea" leads him. Let us believe for a moment his statement that Leninism does "fundamentally contradict Marxism." But what follows? What comes of this? The following. "Leninism carried with it" *Iskra* (the old *Iskra*)—this the author does not deny—consequently *Iskra*, too, "fundamentally contradicts Marxism." The Second Party Congress—the majority, numbering 35 votes—recognised *Iskra* as the central organ of the Party and highly praised its services; consequently, that congress, its programme and its tactics, also "fundamentally contradict Marxism." . . . Funny, isn't it, reader?

The author, nevertheless, continues: "In Lenin's opinion the spontaneous working-class movement is moving towards combination with the bourgeoisie. . . ." Yes, indeed, the author is undoubtedly moving towards combination with idiocy, and it would be a good thing if he digressed from that path.

But let us leave the "critic." Let us turn to Marxism.

Our esteemed "critic" obstinately reiterates that the stand taken by the "majority" and by its representative, Lenin, fundamentally contradicts Marxism, because, he says, Kautsky, Marx and Engels say the opposite of what Lenin advocates! Is that the case? Let us see!

"K. Kautsky," the author informs us, "writes in his *Erfurt Programme:* 'The interests of the proletariat and the bourgeoisie are so antagonistic that the strivings of these two classes cannot be combined for any more or less prolonged period. In every country where the capitalist mode of production prevails the participation of the working class in politics *sooner or later* leads to the working class separating from the bourgeois parties and forming an independent *workers' party.*'"

But what follows from this? Only that the interests of the bourgeoisie and the proletariat are antagonistic, that "sooner or later" the proletariat separates from the bourgeoisie to form an independent *workers' party* (remember: a *workers' party,* but not a *Social-Democratic workers' party*). The author assumes that here Kautsky disagrees with Lenin. But Lenin says that sooner or later the proletariat will not only separate from the bourgeoisie, but will bring about the social revolution, i.e., will overthrow the bourgeoisie. The taskof Social-Democracy — he adds — is to try to make this come about as *quickly* as possible, and to come about *consciously.* Yes, *consciously* and not spontaneously, for it is about this consciousness that Lenin writes.

". . . Where things have reached the stage of the formation of an independent workers' party," continues the "critic," citing Kautsky's book, "the party must sooner or later, of natural necessity, *assimilate* socialist tendencies if it was not inspired by them from the very outset; it must in the long run become a *socialist* workers' party, i.e., *Social-Democracy.*"

What does that mean? Only that the workers' party will *assimilate* socialist trends. But does Lenin deny this? Not in the least! Lenin plainly says that not only the workers' party, but the entire working class assimilates socialism. What, then, is the nonsense we hear from *Social-Democrat* and its prevaricating hero? What is the use of all this balderdash? As the saying goes: He heard the sound of a bell, but where it came from he could

24

not tell. That's exactly what happened to our muddle-headed author.

As you see, Kautsky does not differ one iota from Lenin on that point. But all this reveals the author's thoughtlessness with exceptional clarity.

Does Kautsky say anything in support of the stand taken by the "majority"? Here is what he writes in one of his splendid articles, in which he analyses the draft programme of Austrian Social-Democracy:

"Many of our revisionist critics (the followers of Bernstein) believe that Marx asserted that economic development and the class struggle create not only the conditions for socialist production, but also, and directly, engender the *consciousness (K. Kautsky's italics)* of its necessity. And these critics at once object that Britain, the country most highly developed capi-talistically, is more remote than any other from this consciousness. Judging from the (Austrian) draft, one might assume that this . . . view . . . was shared by the committee that drafted the Austrian programme. In the draft programme it is stated: 'The more capitalist development increases the numbers of the proletariat, the more the proletariat is compelled and becomes fit to fight against capitalism. The proletariat *becomes conscious'* of the possibility of and of the necessity for socialism. In this connection socialist consciousness appears to be a necessary and direct result of the proletarian class struggle. But that is absolutely *untrue.* . . . Modern socialist consciousness can arise *only on the basis of profound scientific knowledge.* . . . The vehicle of science is not the proletariat, but the *bourgeois intelligentsia (K. Kautsky's italics)* . It was in the minds of individual members of that stratum that modern socialism originated, and it was they who communicated it (scientific socialism) to the more intellectually developed proletarians who, in their turn, introduce it into the proletarian class struggle. . . . Thus, socialist consciousness is something *introduced* into the proletarian class struggle *from without* and not something that *arose within it* spontaneously. Accordingly, the old Hainfeld programme quite rightly stated that the task of Social-Democracy is to *imbue the proletariat with the consciousness* of its position and the consciousness of its task . . ."

Do you not recall, reader, analogous thoughts expressed by Lenin on this question; do you not recall the well-known stand taken by the "majority"? Why did the "Tiflis Committee" and its Social-Democrat conceal the truth? Why, in speaking of Kautsky, did our esteemed "critic" fail to quote these words of Kautsky's in his article? Whom are these most highly esteemed gentlemen trying to deceive? Why are they so "contemptuous" towards their readers? Is it not because . . . they fear the truth, hide from the truth, and think that the truth also can be hidden? They behave like the bird which hides its head in the sand and imagines that nobody can see it! But they delude themselves as that bird does.

If socialist consciousness has been worked out on a scientific basis, and if this consciousness is introduced into the working-class movement from without by the efforts of Social-Democracy — it is clear that all this happens because the working class, so long as it remains a working class, cannot lead science and work out scientific socialism by its own efforts: it lacks both the time and the means for this.

Here is what K. Kautsky says in his *Erfurt Programme:*

". . . The proletarian can at best assimilate part of the knowledge worked out by bourgeois learning and adapt it to his objects and needs, but so long as he remains a proletarian he lacks the leisure and means independently to carry science beyond the limits reached by bourgeois thinkers. Hence, spontaneous workers' socialism must bear all the essential marks of utopianism"(utopianism is a false, unscientific theory).

Utopian socialism of this kind often assumes an anarchistic character, continues Kautsky, but ". . . As is well

26

known, wherever the anarchist movement (meaning by that proletarian utopianism — *K. Kautsky*) really permeated the masses and became a class movement it always, sooner or later, despite its seeming radicalism, ended by being transformed into *a purely trade-unionist movement* of the narrowest kind."

In other words, if the working-class movement is not combined with scientific socialism it inevitably becomes petty, assumes a "narrow trade-unionist" character and, consequently, submits to trade-unionist ideology.

"But that means belittling the workers and extolling the intelligentsia!"—howl our "critic" and his *Social-Democrat. . . .* Poor "critic"! Miserable *Social-Democrat!* They take the proletariat for a capricious young lady who must not be told the truth, who must always be paid compliments so that she will not run away! No, most highly esteemed gentlemen! We believe that the proletariat will display more staunchness thanyou think. We believe that it will not fear the truth! As for you. . . . What can one say to you? Even now you have shown that you fear the truth and, in your article, did not tell your readers what Kautsky's real views are. . . .

Thus, scientific socialism *without the working-class movement* is an empty phrase that can always be easily thrown to the winds.

On the other hand, the working-class movement *without socialism* is aimless trade-unionist wandering, which some time or other will, of course, lead to the social revolution, but at the cost of long pain and suffering.

The conclusion?

"The working-class movement must combine with socialism": "Social-Democracy is a combination of the working-class movement with socialism."

That is what Kautsky, the Marxist theoretician, says.

We have seen that *Iskra* (the old *Iskra*) and the

"majority" say the same.

We have seen that Comrade Lenin takes the same stand.

Thus, the "majority" takes a firm Marxist stand.

Clearly, "contempt for the workers," "extolling the intelligentsia," the "un-Marxist stand of the majority," and similar gems which the Menshevik "critics" scatter so profusely, are nothing more than catchwords, figments of the imagination of the Tiflis "Men-sheviks."

On the other hand, we shall see that actually it is the Tiflis "minority," the "Tiflis Committee" and its *Social-Democrat* that "fundamentally contradict Marxism." But of this anon. Meanwhile, we draw attention to the following:

In support of his utterances, the author of the article "Majority or Minority?" quotes the words of Marx (?): "The theoretician of any given class comes theoretically to the conclusion *to which the class itself has already arrived practically.*"

One of two things. Either the author does not know the Georgian language, or else there is a printer's error. No literate person would say *"to which it has already arrived."* It would be correct to say: *"at which it has already arrived,"* or *"to which it is already coming."* If the author had in mind the latter *(to which it is already coming)*, then I must observe that he is misquoting Marx; Marx did not say anything of the kind. If the author had the first formula in mind, then the sentence he quoted should have run as follows: "The theoretician of any given class arrives theoretically at the conclusion at which the class itself *has already arrived practically."* In other words, since Marx and Engels arrived theoretically at the conclusion that the collapse of capitalism and the building of socialism are inevitable — it implies that the proletariat *has already* rejected capitalism *practically,* has already crushed capitalism and has built up the socialist way of life in its place!

Poor Marx! Who knows how many more absurdities our

pseudo-Marxists will ascribe to him?

But did Marx really say that? Here is what he actually said: The theoreticians who represent the petty bourgeoisie "are . . . *driven, theoretically, to the same problems and solutions to which* material interest and social position *drive the latter practically.* This is, in general, the relationship between the political and literary representatives of a class and the class they represent."

As you see, Marx does not say *"already arrived to."* These "philosophical" words were invented by our esteemed "critic."

Consequently Marx's own words possess an entirely different meaning.

What idea does Marx propound in the above-quoted proposition? Only that the theoretician of a given class *cannot create* an ideal, the elements of which do not exist in life; that he can *only indicate* the elements of the future and on that basis theoretically create an ideal which the given class reaches practically. The difference is that the theoretician runs ahead of the class and indicates the embryo of the future before the class does. That is what is meant by "arriving at something theoretically."

Here is what Marx and Engels say in their *Manifesto*: "The Communists (i.e., Social-Democrats), therefore, are on the one hand, practically, the most advanced and resolute section of the working-class parties of every country, that section which *pushes forward* all others; on the other hand, theoretically, they have over the great mass of the proletariat the advantage of *clearly understanding* the line of march, the conditions, and the ultimate *general* results of the proletarian movement."

Yes, the ideologists *"push forward,"* they see much farther than the "great mass of the proletariat," and this is the whole point. The ideologists push forward, and it is precisely for this reason that the idea, socialist consciousness, is of such great importance for the movement.

Is that why you attack the "majority," esteemed "critic"? If it is, then say good-bye to Marxism, and know that the "majority" is proud of its Marxist stand.

The situation of the "majority" in this case in many ways recalls that of Engels in the nineties.

The idea is the source of social life, asserted the idealists. In their opinion, social consciousness is the foundation upon which the life of society is built. That is why they were called idealists.

It had to be proved that ideas do not drop from the skies, but are engendered by life itself.

Marx and Engels entered the historical arena and magnificently accomplished this task. They proved that social life is the source of ideas and, therefore, that the life of society is the foundation on which social consciousness is built. Thereby, they dug the grave of idealism and cleared the road for materialism.

Certain semi-Marxists interpreted this as meaning that consciousness, ideas, are of very little importance in life.

The great importance of ideas had to be proved. And so Engels came forward and, in his letters (1891-94), emphasised that while it is true that ideas do not drop from the skies but are engendered by life itself, yet once born, ideas acquire great importance, for they unite men, organise them, and put their impress upon the social life which has engendered them—ideas are of great importance in historical progress.

"This is not Marxism but the betrayal of Marxism," shouted Bernstein and his ilk. The Marxists only laughed.

There were semi-Marxists in Russia—the "Economists." They asserted that, since ideas are engendered by social life, socialist consciousness is of little importance for the working-class movement.

It had to be proved that socialist consciousness is of great importance for the working-class movement, that without it the movement would be aimless trade-unionist wandering, and nobody could say when the proletariat would rid itself of it and reach the social revolution.

And *Iskra* appeared and magnificently accomplished this task. The book *What Is To Be Done?* appeared, in which Lenin emphasised the great importance of socialist consciousness. The Party "majority" was formed and firmly took this path.

But here the little Bernsteins come out and begin to shout: This "fundamentally contradicts Marxism"!

But do you, little "Economists," know what Marxism is?

* * *

Surprising!—the reader will say. What's the matter? — he will ask. Why did Plekhanov write his article criticising Lenin (see the new *Iskra*, Nos. 10, 11)? Whatis he censuring the "majority" for? Are not the pseudo-Marxists of Tiflis and their *Social-Democrat* repeating the ideas expressed by Plekhanov? Yes, they are repeating them, but in such a clumsy way that it becomes disgusting. Yes, Plekhanov did criticise. But do you know what the point is? Plekhanov does not disagree with the "majority" and with Lenin. And not only Plekhanov. Neither Martov, nor Zasulich, nor Axelrod disagree with them. Actually, on the question we have been discussing, the leaders of the "minority" do not disagree with the old *Iskra*. And the old *Iskra* is the banner of the "majority." Don't be surprised! Here are the facts:

We are familiar with the old *Iskra*' s programmatic article (see above). We know that that article fully expresses the stand taken by the "majority." Whose article is it? The article of the editorial board of *Iskra* of that time. Who were the members of that editorial board? Lenin, Plekhanov, Axelrod, Martov, Zasulich and Sta-rover. Of these only Lenin now belongs to the "majority"; the other five are the leaders of the "minority"; but the fact remains that they were the editors of *Iskra'*s programmatic article, consequently, they ought not to repudiate their own words; presumably they believed what they wrote.

But we shall leave *Iskra* if you like.

Here is what Martov writes:

"Thus, the idea of socialism first arose not among the masses of the workers, but in the studies of scholars from the ranks of the bourgeoisie."

And here is what Vera Zasulich writes:

"Even the idea of the class solidarity of the entire proletariat . . . is not so simple that it could arise independently in the mind of every worker. . . . And socialism . . . most certainly does not spring up in the minds of the workers 'automatically.' . . . The ground for the theory of socialism was prepared by the entire development of both life and knowledge . . . and created by the mind of a genius who was armed with that knowledge. Similarly, the dissemination of the ideas of socialism among the workers was initiated, almost over the entire continent of Europe, by Socialists who had received their training in educational establishments for the upper classes."

Let us now hear Plekhanov, who so pompously and solemnly criticises Lenin in the new *Iskra* (Nos. 10, 11). The scene is the Second Party Congress. Plekhanov is arguing against Martynov and defending Lenin. He censures Martynov, who had seized on a single sentence of Lenin's and had overlooked the book *What Is To Be Done?* as a whole, and goes on to say:

"Comrade Martynov's trick reminds me of a censor who said: 'Permit me to tear a sentence from the Lord's Prayer from its context and I will prove to you that its author deserves to be hanged.' But all the reproaches hurled at this unfortunate sentence (Lenin's) not only by Comrade Martynov but also by many, many others, are based on a misunderstanding. Comrade Martynov quotes the words of Engels: 'Modern socialism is the theoretical expression of the modern working-class movement.'

Comrade Lenin also agrees with Engels. . . . But Engels's words are a general proposition. The question is, who first formulates this theoretical expression? Lenin did not write a treatise on the philosophy of history but a polemical article against the 'Economists,' who said: we must wait and see what the working class arrives at by its own efforts without the aid of the 'revolutionary bacillus' (i.e., without Social-Democracy) . The latter was prohibited from telling the workers anything, precisely because it is a 'revolutionary bacillus,' i.e., because it possesses theoretical consciousness. But if you eliminate the 'bacillus,' all that remains is the unconscious mass, into which consciousness must be introduced from outside. Had you wanted to be fair to Lenin, and had you carefully read his whole book, you would have seen that that is precisely what he says." That is what Plekhanov said at the Second Party Congress.

And now, several months later, the same Plekhanov, instigated by the same Martov, Axelrod, Zasulich, Starover and others, speaks again, and seizing on the very same sentence of Lenin's that he *defended* at the congress, says: Lenin and the "majority" are not Marxists. He knows that even if a sentence from the Lord's Prayer is torn from its context and interpreted separately, the author of the Prayer might find himself on the gallows for heresy. He knows that this would be unfair, that an unbiassed critic would not do such a thing; nevertheless, he tears this sentence from Lenin's book; nevertheless he acts unfairly, and publicly besmirches himself. And Martov, Zasulich, Axelrod and Starover pander to him and publish his article under their editorship in the new *Iskra* (Nos. 70, 71), and thereby disgrace themselves once again.

Why did they exhibit such spinelessness? Why did these

leaders of the "minority" besmirch themselves? Why did they repudiate the programmatic article in *Iskra* to which they themselves had subscribed? Why did they repudiate their own words? Has such falsity ever before been heard of in the Social-Democratic Party?

What happened during the few months that elapsed between the Second Congress and the appearance of Plekhanov's article?

What happened was this: Of the six editors, the Second Congress elected only three to be editors of *Iskra*: Plekhanov, Lenin and Martov. As for Axelrod, Starover and Zasulich—the congress appointed them to other posts. It goes without saying that the congress had a right to do this, and it was the duty of everyone to submit to it; the congress expresses the will of the Party, it is the supreme organ of the Party, and whoever acts contrary to its decisions tramples upon the will of the Party.

But these obstinate editors did not submit to the will of the Party, to Party discipline (Party discipline is the same as the will of the Party). It would appear that Party discipline was invented only for simple Party workers like us! They were angry with the congress for not electing them as editors; they stepped to the side, took Martov with them, and formed an opposition. They proclaimed a boycott against the Party, refused to carry on any Party activities and began to threaten the Party. Elect us, they said, to the editorial board, tothe Central Committee and to the Party Council, otherwise we shall cause a split. And a split ensued. Thus they trampled upon the will of the Party once again. Here are the demands of the striker-editors: "The old editorial board of *Iskra* to be restored (i.e., give us three seats on the editorial board).

"A definite number of members of the opposition (i.e., of the "minority") to be installed in the Central Committee.

"Two seats in the Party Council to be allocated to members of the opposition, etc. . . . .

"We present these terms as the only ones that will enable the Party to avoid a conflict which will threaten its very existence" (i.e., satisfy our demands, otherwise we shall cause a big split in the Party).

What did the Party say to them in reply?

The Party's representative, the Central Committee, and other comrades said to them: We cannot go against the decisions of the Party congress; elections are a matter for the congress; nevertheless, we shall endeavour to restore peace and harmony, although, to tell the truth, it is disgraceful to fight *for seats;* you want to split the Party *for the sake of seats,* etc.

The striker-editors took offence; they were embarrassed — indeed, it did look as though they had started the fight for the sake of seats; they pulled Plekhanov over to their side and launched their heroic cause.

They were obliged to seek some *"stronger" "disagreement"* between the "majority" and "minority" in order to show that they were not fighting for the sake of seats. They searched and searched until they found a passage in Lenin's book which, if torn from the context and interpreted separately, could indeed be cavilled at. A happy idea—thought the leaders of the "minority" — Lenin is the leader of the "majority," let us discredit Lenin and thereby swing the Party to our side. And so Plekhanov began to trumpet to the world that "Lenin and his followers are not Marxists." True, only yesterday they defended the very idea in Lenin's book which they are attacking today, but that cannot be helped; anopportunist is called an opportunist precisely because he has no respect for principle.

That is why they besmirch themselves; that is the cause of their falsity.

But that is not all.

Some time passed. They saw that nobody was paying attention to their agitation against the "majority" and Lenin, apart from a few naive persons. They saw that their "affairs" were in a bad way and decided to change their colours again. On March 10, 1905, the same Plekhanov, and the same Martov and Axelrod, in the name of the Party Council, passed a resolution in which, among other things, they said:

"Comrades! (addressing themselves to the "majority"). . . . Both sides (i.e., the "majority" and the "minority") have repeatedly expressed the conviction that the existing disagreements on tactics and organisation are not of such a character as to render impossible activities within a single Party organisation"; therefore, they said, let us convene a comrades' court (consisting of Bebel and others) to settle our slight disagreement.

In short, the disagreements in the Party are merely a squabble, which a comrades' court will investigate, but we are a united whole.

But how can that be? We "non-Marxists" are invited into the Party organisations, we are a united whole, and so on and so forth. . . . What does it mean? Why, you leaders of the "minority" are betraying the Party! Can "non-Marxists" be put at the head of the Party? Is there room for "non-Marxists" in the ranks of the Social-Democratic Party? Or, perhaps, you, too, have betrayed the cause of Marxism and have, therefore, changed front?

But it would be naive to expect a reply. The point is that these wonderful leaders have several "principles" in their pockets, and whenever they want a particular one they take it out. As the saying goes: They have a different opinion for every day in the week! . . .

Such are the leaders of the so-called "minority."

It is easy to picture to oneself what the tail of this leadership—the so-called Tiflis "minority"—is like. . . . The trouble also is that at times the tail pays no heed to the head and refuses to obey. For example, while the leaders of the "minority" consider that conciliation is possible and call for harmony among the Party workers, the Tiflis "minority" and its *Social-Democrat* continue to rave and shout: between the "majority" and "minority" there is "a life-and-death struggle"; we must exterminate each other! They are all at sixes and sevens.

The "minority" complain that we call them opportunist (unprincipled). But what else can we call them if they repudiate their own words, if they swing from side to side, if they are eternally wavering and hesitating? Can a genuine Social-Democrat change his opinions every now and again? The "minority" change theirs more often than one changes pocket handkerchiefs.

Our pseudo-Marxists obstinately reiterate that the "minority" is truly proletarian in character. Is that so? Let us see.

Kautsky says that "it is easier for the proletarian to become imbued with Party principles, he inclinestowards a principled policy that is independent of the mood of the moment and of personal or local interests."

But what about the "minority"? Is it inclined towards a policy that is independent of the mood of the moment, etc.? On the contrary: it is always hesitating, eternally wavering; it detests a firm principled policy, it prefers unprincipledness; it follows the mood of the moment. We are already familiar with the facts.

Kautsky says that the proletarian likes Party discipline: "The proletarian is a nonentity so long as he remains an isolated individual. His strength, his progress, his hopes and expectations are entirely derived from *organisation*. . . . " That is why he is not distracted by personal advantage or personal glory; he "performs his duty in any post he is assigned to with a voluntary discipline which pervades all his feelings and thoughts."

But what about the "minority"? Is it, too, imbued with a

37

sense of discipline? On the contrary, it despises Party discipline and ridicules it. The first to set an example in violating Party discipline were the leaders of the "minority." Recall Axelrod, Zasulich, Starover, Martov and others, who refused to submit to the decision of the Second Congress.

"Quite different is the case of the intellectual," continues Kautsky. He finds it extremely difficult to submit to Party discipline and does so by compulsion, not of his own free will. "He recognises the need of discipline only for the mass, not for the chosen few. And of course, he counts himself among these few. . . . An ideal example of an intellectual who had become thoroughly imbued with the sentiments of the proletariat, and who . . . worked in any post he was assigned to, subordinated himself whole-heartedly to our great cause, and despised the spineless whining . . . which the intellectual . . . is all too prone to indulge in when he happens to be in the minority—an ideal example of such an intellectual . . . was Liebknecht. We may also mention Marx, who never forced himself to the forefront and whose Party discipline in the International, where he often found himself in the minority, was exemplary."

But what about the "minority"? Does it display anything of the "sentiments of the proletariat"? Is its conduct anything like that of Liebknecht and Marx? On the contrary, we have seen that the leaders of the "minority" have not subordinated their "ego" to our sacred cause; we have seen that it was these leaders who indulged in "spineless whining when they found themselves in the minority" at the Second Congress; we have seen that it was they who, after the congress, wailed for "front seats," and that it was they who started a Party split for the sake of these seats. . . .

Is this your "proletarian character," esteemed Mensheviks?

Then why are the workers on our side in some towns? the Mensheviks ask us.

Yes, it is true, in some towns the workers are on the side of the "minority," but that proves nothing. Workers even follow the revisionists (the opportunists in Germany) in some towns, but that does not prove that their stand is a proletarian one; it does not prove that they are not opportunists. One day a crow found a rose, but that did not prove that a crow is a nightingale. It is not for nothing that the saying goes:

When   a   crow   picks   up   a   rose
"I'm a nightingale," it crows.

It is now clear *on what grounds* the disagreements in the Party arose. As is evident, two trends have appeared in our Party: the trend of *proletarian firmness,* and the trend of *intellectual wavering.* And this intellectual wavering is expressed by the present "minority." The Tiflis "Committee" and its *Social-Democrat* are the obedient slaves of this "minority"!

That is the whole point.

True, our pseudo-Marxists often shout that they are opposed to the "mentality of the intellectual," and they accuse the "majority" of "intellectual wavering"; but this reminds us of the case of the thief who stole some money and began to shout: "Stop thief!"

Moreover, it is well known that the tongue ever turns to the aching tooth.

Also available from the publisher:

Selected Works of Salvador Allende

Ethics of Socialism - Ernest Belfort Bax

Twenty Years in Underground Russia – Cecilia Bobrovskaya

The Decline of American Capitalism – Lewis Corey

Imperialism and the Revolution – Enver Hoxha

The Selected Works of Kim Il Sung

The Stalin Era - Anna Louise Strong

www.PrismKeyPress.com